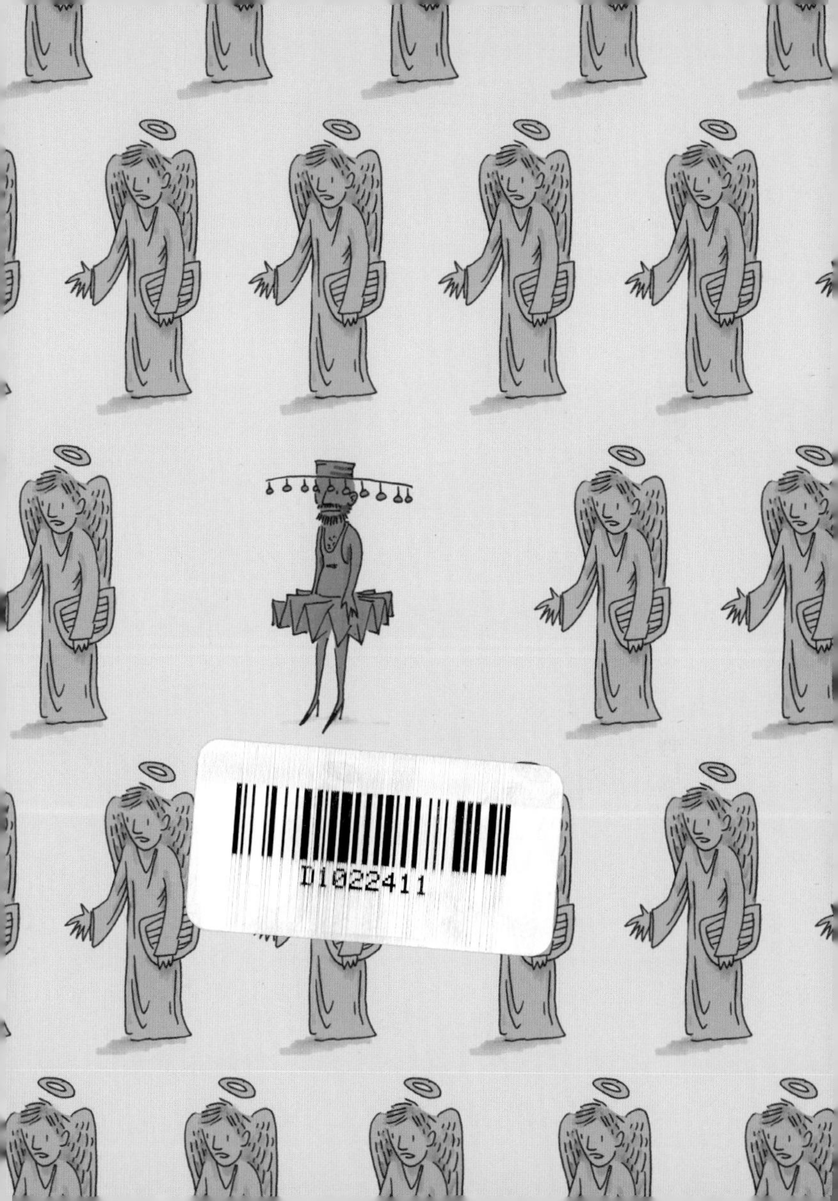

I Told You So

---◆---

Special Thanks:

Patricia Wheeler, Richard Epstein, Rani Viva, Chip Mosher,
Austin, Berkeley, Ariel, Maria and Max.
And Matt Diffee and Bob Mankoff at *The New Yorker*.

I TOLD YOU SO
Published by BOOM! Town,
An imprint of BOOM! Studios.

Office of Publication
6310 San Vicente Boulevard, Suite 107
Los Angeles, CA 90048-5457

A catalog record for this book is available from OCLC and from the BOOM! Studios
website, www.boom-studios.com, on the Librarians page.

More information about Shannon Wheeler and his work can be found on his website:
www.tmcm.com
You can contact Shannon Wheeler at: cartoons@tmcm.com

FIRST HARDCOVER EDITION
April 2012
ISBN: 978-1-60886-093-7

Assistant Editor: Adam Staffaroni
Book Design: Danielle Keller

I Told You So

SHANNON WHEELER
Introduction by MATTHEW DIFFEE

BOOM! Town is an imprint of BOOM! Studios

❧ INTRODUCTION ❧

A lot of people think Shannon Wheeler is some kind of creative genius. That, I assure you, is not the case. You see, most cartoonists, myself included, work really hard all day long trying to come up with ideas for cartoons. But not Mr. Wheeler. His material comes straight from real life. Take the cartoon on page 110. That really happened, exactly like Shannon recorded it here. I know this for a fact because I was there.

It was eight years ago. Shannon and I had just polished off a rack of yak ribs at this little gem of a BBQ joint tucked into the Sivalik Hills in Nepal. We were there on business, trekking west to meet with the editors of a nascent Pakistani humor magazine called The Gujranwala Monthly (known affectionately in the 'toon biz as the Paki Gag Rag; sadly it didn't last through the downturn). Anyway, as we were considering the dessert menu, a handful of space aliens came in, four or five of them, completely nude (if you must know, they're like humans, but in triplicate). One of them made a beeline for the dark end of the bar and kept pestering this depressed yeti with questions. He wouldn't let up and eventually the big fella got so upset he hauled off and socked the alien in the forehead with one of his tiny fists. (That's something a lot of people don't know about yetis; big feet, small hands. And it's further proof that Wheeler isn't very imaginative. If he was making it up, don't you think he would have drawn the hands the size that most people incorrectly assume them to be? Yes, he would.)

Well, at this point, as a trickle of blue goop oozed out of the alien's nose, all his buddies grabbed their brain-tasers and started swinging them around willy-nilly and things escalated real quick. A gang of plastered Leprechauns scrambled for their magic daggers and Elvis, who I hadn't even noticed until then, pulled out a crossbow. Wheeler and I were unarmed, so he wet his pants while I fashioned nunchaku from a pair of still-connected yak bones. It was a pretty tense standoff for several slow moments until, luckily, a unicorn farted and everyone laughed. Anyway, the point is, this caption you see underneath that cartoon was spoken word for word by the alien. Shannon didn't invent squat. I would have jotted it down myself except that Shannon called dibs while I was distracted asking the waiter if the turnip cheesecake was homemade.

Now, should we appreciate the gags in this book less because they are mere recordings of true events? Absolutely not. They are delightful regardless of how easy they were to produce. Should we admire Mr. Wheeler a little less and admire other cartoonists like myself who actually come up with ideas a little bit more? Sure, why not?

—MATTHEW DIFFEE
New Yorker Cartoonist

San Francisco

"I lost everything when I lost my cell phone."

San Francisco

"Cream is self-serve."

San Francisco

"I'm not hip, but I am hipper-than-thou."

"*I can't decide if it's funny because they're cartoons or if it's serious because they're art.*"

San Francisco

"*It might be the alcohol talking,
but I don't think you look
like a dog.*"

San Francisco

"And it is said, he who pulls the pen
from the book shall have a bestseller."

13

"So, how long have you been a cat?"

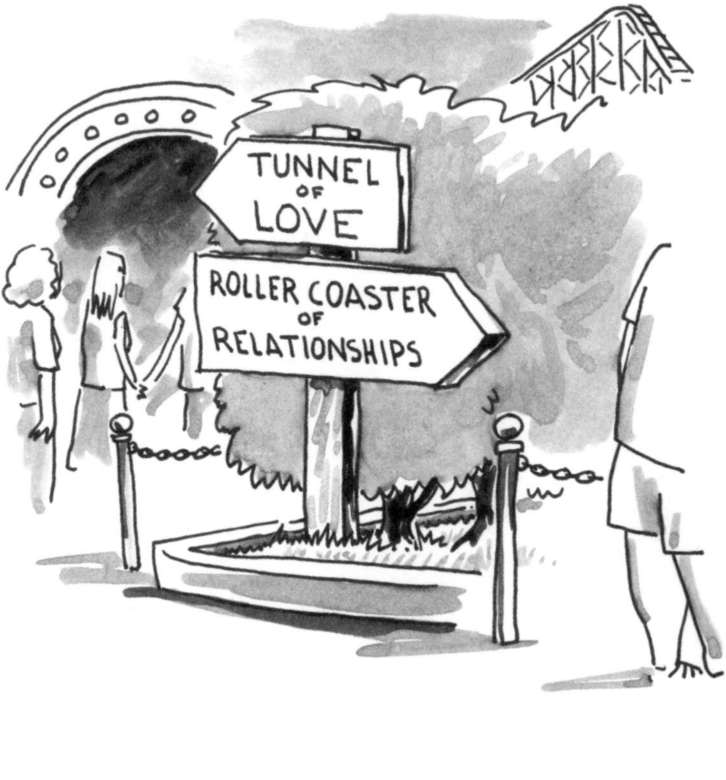
TUNNEL OF LOVE
ROLLER COASTER OF RELATIONSHIPS

15

San Francisco

"Do you mind if I put your cat out?"

San Francisco

*"I'll have years of quiet suffering
and she'll have a regrettable
affair, and then we'll share a
financially devastating divorce."*

San Francisco

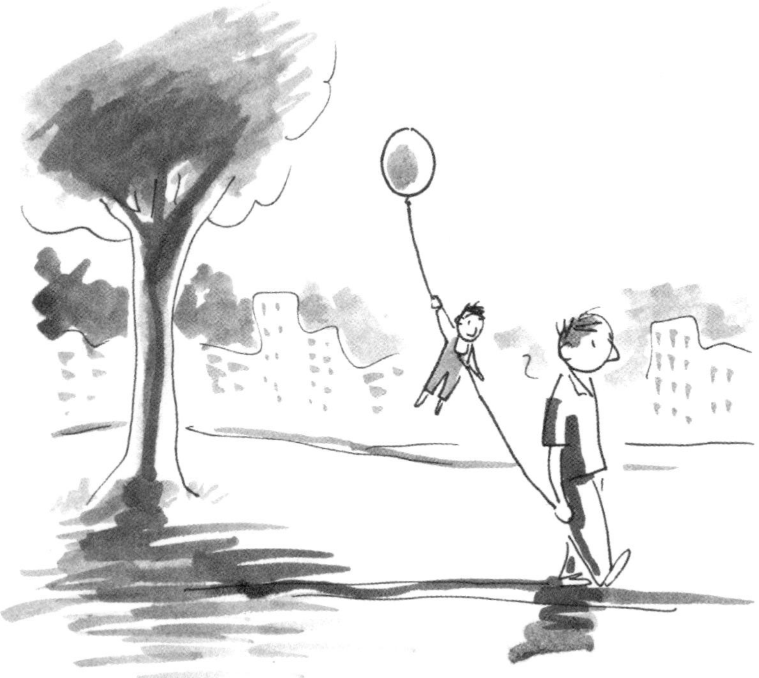

18

San Francisco

"He's a great blend, but he needs a
couple more years to mellow."

San Francisco

*"I take back what I said
about those dog training classes."*

"I'm a sadist trapped in
a masochist's lifestyle."

San Francisco

"Not now. I'm working on my children's book."

San Francisco

"*Comics aren't as fun when
it's called literature.*"

23

"*We're friends without benefits.*"

San Francisco

"*If ignorance is bliss then why
are the ignorant so angry?*"

25

San Francisco

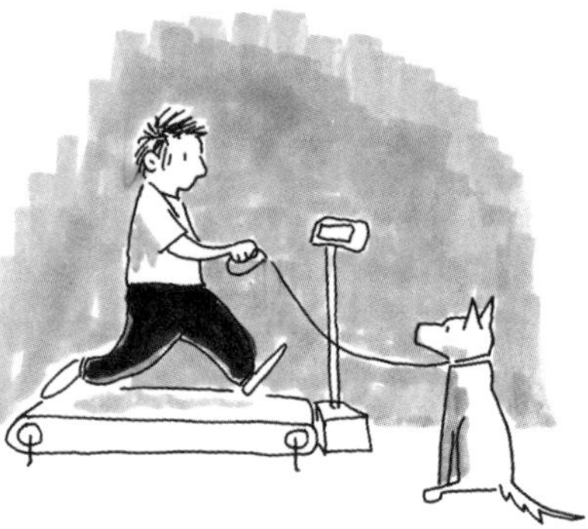

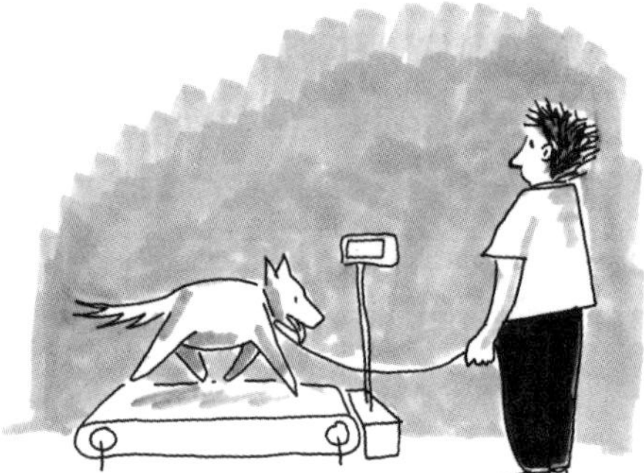

26

San Francisco

New York

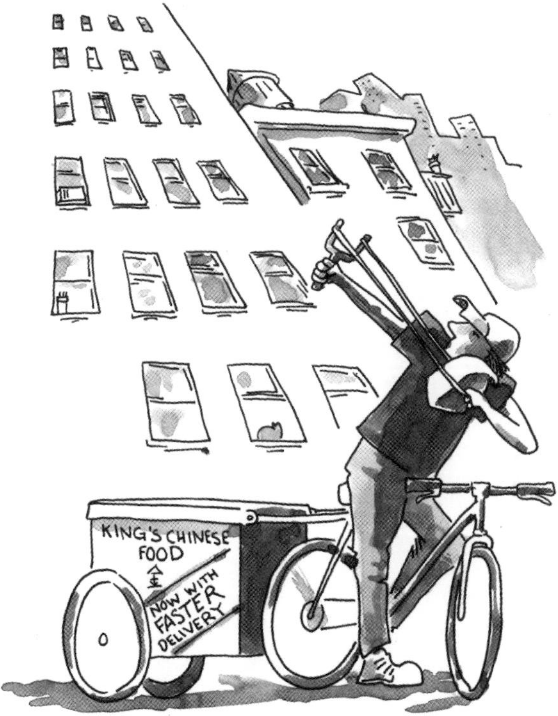
KING'S CHINESE FOOD
NOW WITH FASTER DELIVERY

*"Commuting was easier
before the Sisyphus fad."*

"He's an amazing non-story teller."

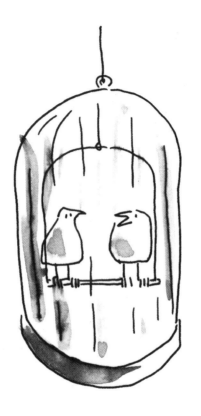

"I'm seeing someone else."

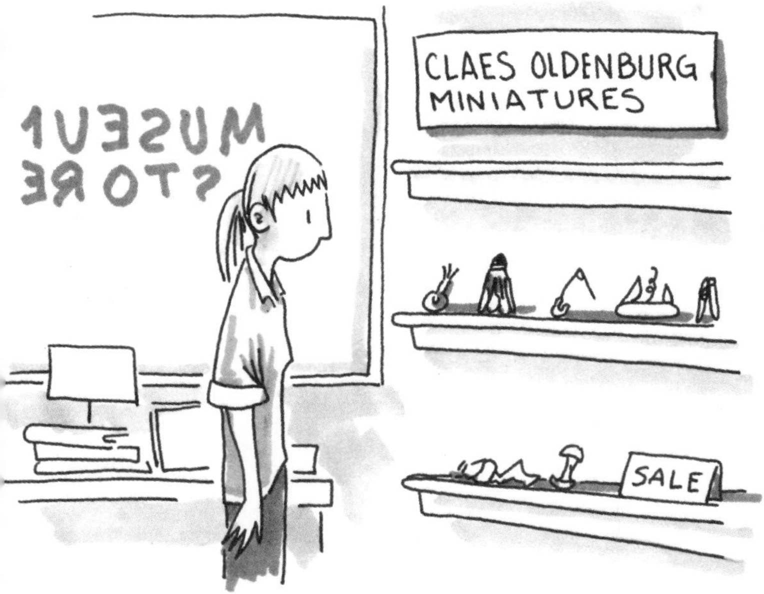
MUSEUM STORE
CLAES OLDENBURG MINIATURES
SALE

"*What's the word for not being able to think of a word?*"

"Gentlemen, we need to refocus
our efforts on the youth market."

"We grew everything ourselves."

*"The older I get, the less time I have,
and the more I plan for the future."*

"This next song is about my
profound loneliness."

"I'm going back to dog walking."

New York

"*Is this your first time in counseling?*"

"This is Matthew Bart Williams III, he'll be conducting our dinner this evening."

"If he's so humble
why haven't I heard of him?"

New York

"Wait, you're an undercover agent, too?"

"I'd like to tell you about our noodling special."

"*Mother shall have parenting time every Thursday night ending the following Monday morning. In even-numbered years, she shall have parenting time on Thanksgiving and Father will have parenting time on Easter Day, while each will have two uninterrupted weeks during each summer vacation. And that takes care of the dog. Now for the cat...*"

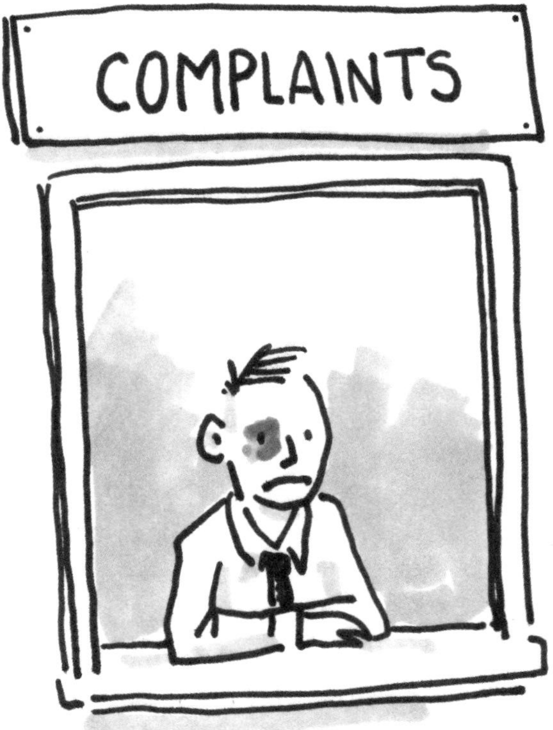
COMPLAINTS

"Your table is ready."

New York

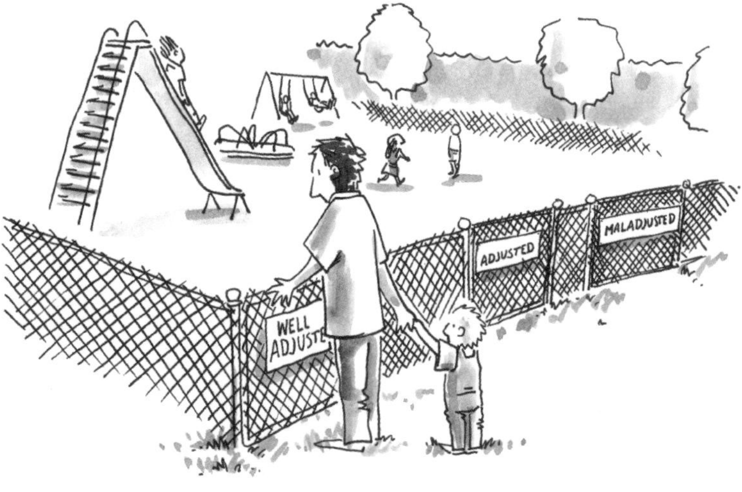
WELL ADJUSTE
ADJUSTED
MALADJUSTED

New York

Portland

"I don't need them, but they make me look smarter."

Portland

"I believe in marriage the way
the Bible intended - a union between
a man and several women."

Portland

"*No. Your beard doesn't make you look stupid.*"

Portland

"Great. Now we have to put up a
'No Knife Juggling' sign."

Portland

"WYSIWYG!"

"Bees were too expensive. I got flies."

*"We dress him post-materialist punk
though he leans neo-emo."*

*"When people started wearing earplugs
we had to start playing louder."*

"I'd like to know if this
self-medication is right for me."

*"One-third of my friends polled do not
believe your apology is sincere."*

Portland

"I recommend the bass."

I wish more people knew I was famous.

"*I licked everywhere and I still can't find my G-spot.*"

"I shouldn't have gotten my hopes up when you said your cat can cook."

"*Where do you keep your books on shoplifting?*"

"*I hate capitalism and its incessant need for money.*"

"I'm waiting for my reputation
to catch up with my self-image."

"Apathy is the purest expression of my anger."

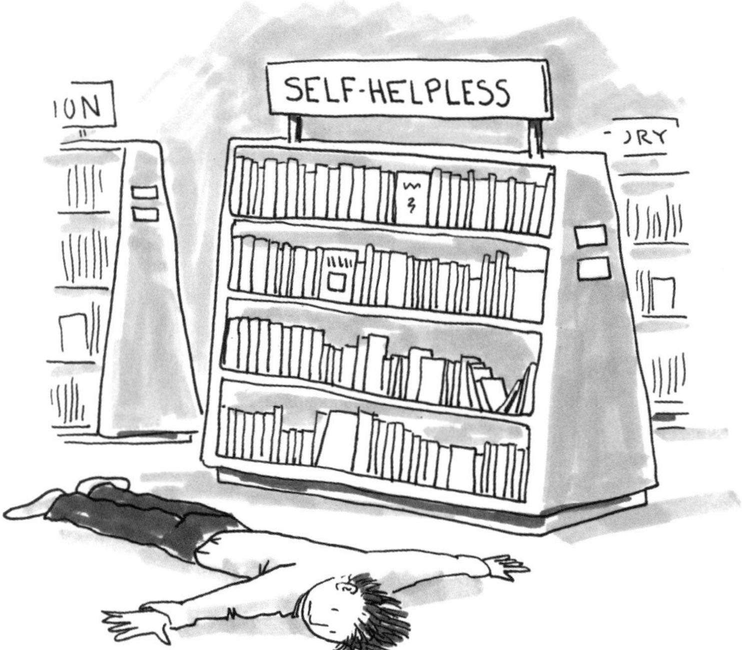
SELF-HELPLESS
ION
ORY

Portland

The Suburbs

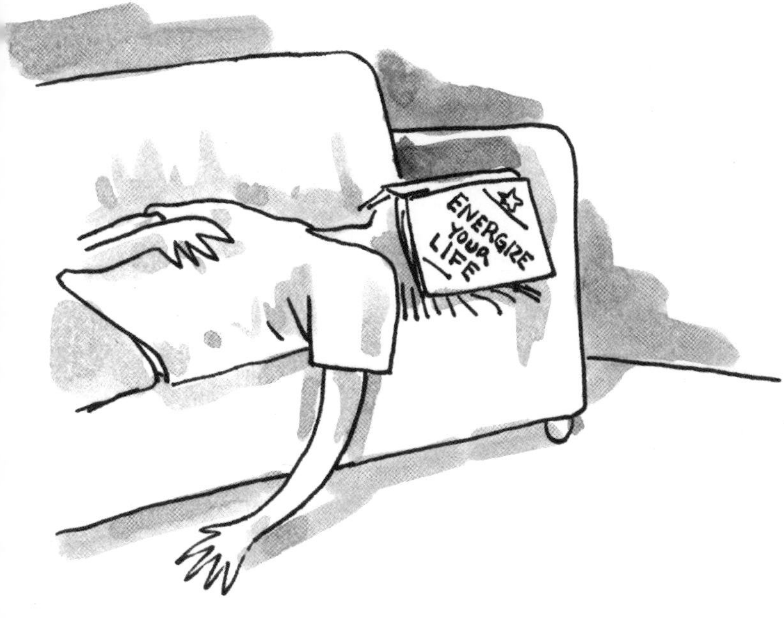
ENERGIZE YOUR LIFE

"*Perhaps I should have been clearer
when I asked for a babysitter
good with discipline.*"

The Suburbs

"I see why you're confused.
I'm wearing the shirt,
but I'm not actually Superman."

The Suburbs

"You're getting fat."

The Suburbs

"At least he's taking requests."

The Suburbs

"No matter how tired I am, I always have the energy to procrastinate."

The Suburbs

*"I brought a prenup if
you want to play house."*

"He wants you to press
play on his audiobook."

The Suburbs

"Can anyone reach the food?"

The Suburbs

"Power corrupts."

"A virus ate my homework."

"You're with child."

"*Three is the new two.*"

The Suburbs

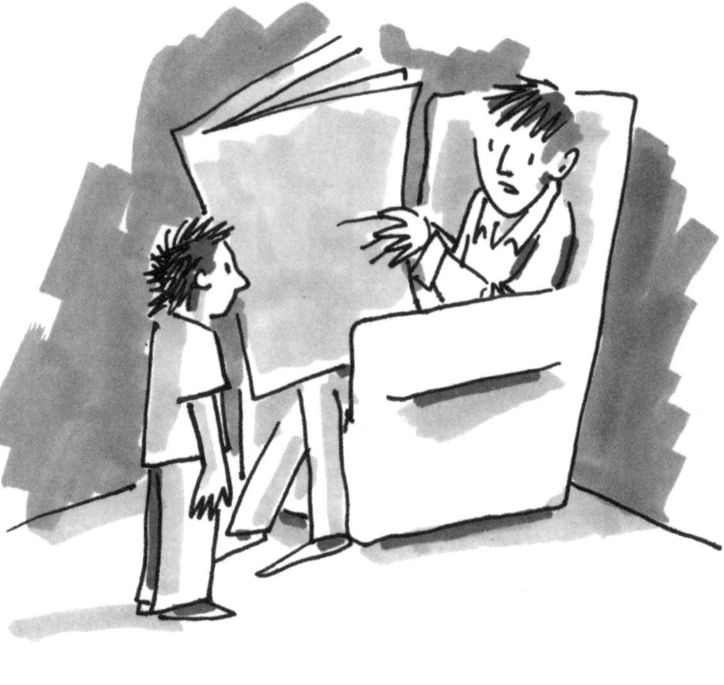

"It's a newspaper."

"You're ruining my napcation."

The Suburbs

*"Could you please stop sitting in my chair,
smoking my pipe, reading my newspaper,
and holding hands with my wife?"*

The Suburbs

"She misses the fish."

The Suburbs

"Infinity bottles of beer on the wall
Infinity bottles of beer
Take one down, pass it around
Infinity bottles of beer on the wall
Infinity bottles of beer
Take one down, pass it around
Infinity bottles of beer on the wall
Infinity bottles of beer
Take one down, pass it around
Infinity bottles of beer on the wall
Infinity bottles of beer
Take one down, pass it around..."

84

"Your move."

The Suburbs

"You lost weight!"

The Internets

APOLOGIES TO
P. STEINER

"*Stupid WikiLeaks.
Now everyone knows I'm a dog.*"

"I don't know about you - but I love the Kindle."

"You're cuter than your profile."

The Internets

"Book club was cancelled when we lost internet."

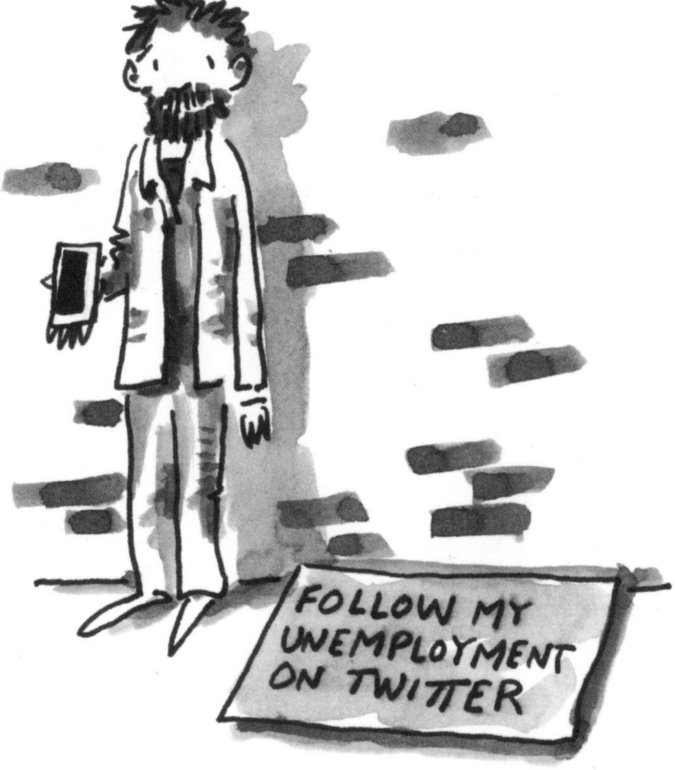
FOLLOW MY UNEMPLOYMENT ON TWITTER

"Thank God you're here! My battery is almost dead."

The Internets

*"You haven't changed a bit since
I saw your Facebook page yesterday!"*

The Internets

*"My purchases were virtual
but my poverty is real."*

"He doesn't surf, he wades."

"Do you want to watch a virtual sunset together?"

The Internets

Unexplored Places

"Finally!"

*"Of course I'm bisexual,
I can't tell anyone apart."*

Unexplored Places

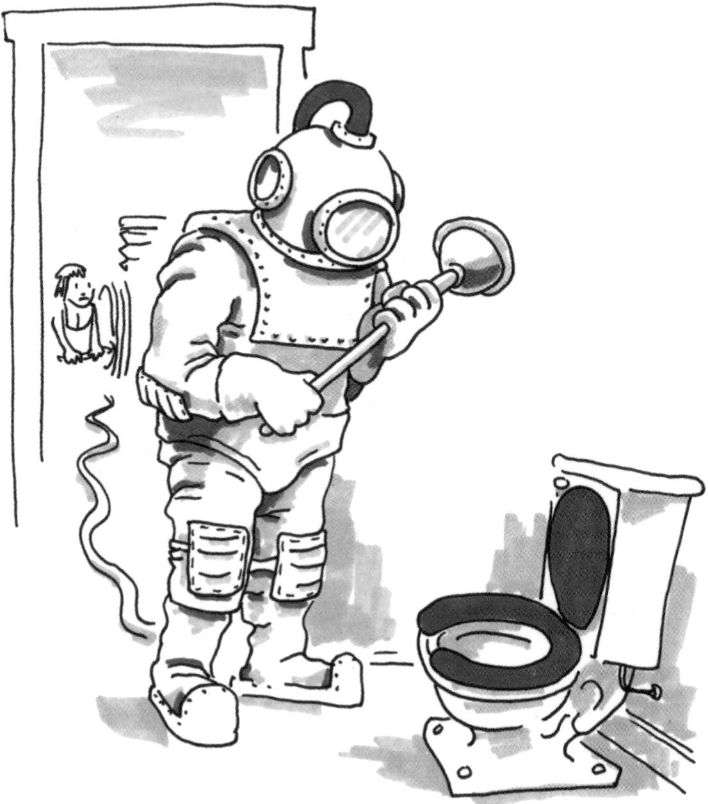

"I can't believe you forgot my birthday."

Unexplored Places

"Cheating on an ethics test
is a double fail."

Unexplored Places

*"It's fine, as long as we don't see
people with dogs on their heads."*

Unexplored Places

"I wish I hadn't believed in reincarnation in my last life."

Unexplored Places

"Happy Pig Day."

105

"Don't worry, I speak opera."

Unexplored Places

"First, let's address your anxiety
and then let's work on that maze."

Unexplored Places

*Cats don't get presents because
Santa Cat sleeps through Christmas.*

Unexplored Places

*"Bartender, there's a tiny man
writing a novel in my beer."*

Unexplored Places

"I've never met the Loch Ness Monster.
Why do you ask?"

Unexplored Places

BLIND SPOT

Unexplored Places

"*Tell me again about evolution.*"

Unexplored Places

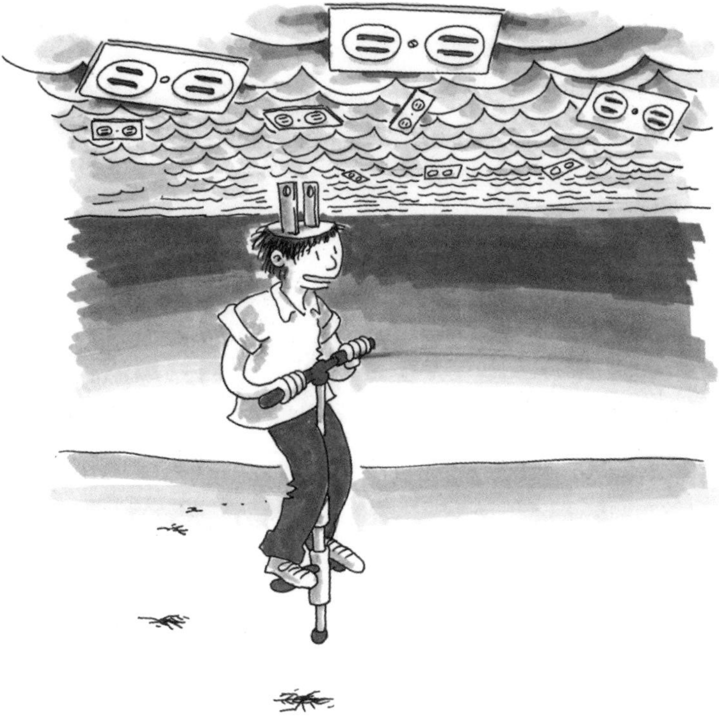

113

Unexplored Places

"*I'm not writing to look like I'm writing.*
I'm writing to write."

Unexplored Places

Unexplored Places

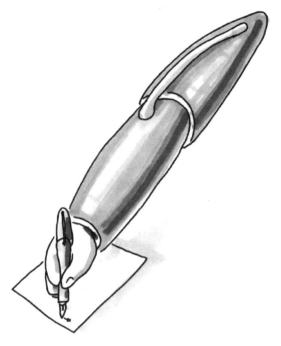

Running wild with an unused degree in architecture, Shannon Wheeler lives in Portland, Oregon where he has cartooned for magazines such as *The New Yorker* and *The Onion*. He's best known for his creation Too Much Coffee Man. More information about and work by Shannon Wheeler can be found at his website: www.tmcm.com.

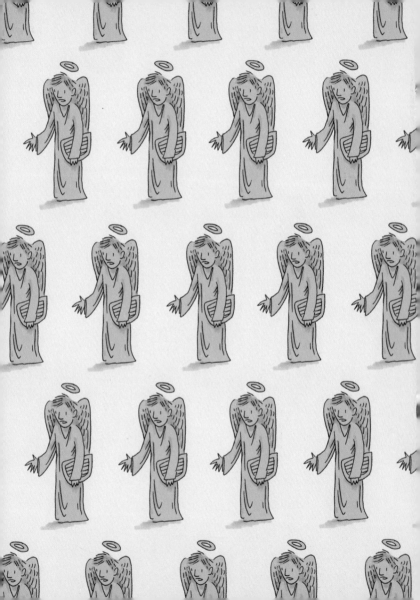